LETTERS HOME from ISRAEL

Marcia S. Gresko

BLACKBIRCH PRESS, INC.

WOODBRIDGE, CONNECTICUT

Published by Blackbirch Press, Inc.
260 Amity Road
Woodbridge, CT 06525

©1999 by Blackbirch Press, Inc.
First Edition

e-mail: staff@blackbirch.com
Web site: www.blackbirch.com

Printed in Singapore

10 9 8 7 6 5 4 3 2 1

All photographs ©Corel Corporation

Library of Congress Cataloging-in-Publication Data
Gresko, Marcia S.
Israel / by Marcia S. Gresko.
    p.   cm. — (Letters home from . . .)
Includes bibliographical references and index.
Summary: Describes some of the sights and experiences on a trip to Israel, including visits to Jerusalem, Bethlehem, Tel Aviv-Jaffa, Haifa, and Nazareth.
ISBN 1-56711-404-0
1. Israel—Juvenile literature. [1. Israel—Description and travel.] I. Title. II. Series.
DS118.G877   1999   98-10913
956.94—dc21   CIP
                                                                             AC

TABLE OF CONTENTS

Arrival in . . .

Jerusalem

Shalom (hello) from Israel! Our bus rolled into Jerusalem at sunrise. What a sight! The round, gold-covered roofs and white stone buildings looked like they came out of a fairy tale.

Jerusalem is in the middle of Israel. It's in the part of the world known as the Middle East. Egypt, Jordan, Syria, and Lebanon are all neighbors.

Our tour guide told us that Israel is a tiny country. She says it's a little larger than the state of New Jersey. Only 5 million people live in Israel. That's less than the number of people who live in New York City! She also explained that Israel is an ancient land, but a new country. It officially became an independent nation just over 50 years ago.

Jerusalem

Visiting Jerusalem is like traveling to two cities at once!

The western part of the city is called the New City. It's mostly modern. It has wide streets, quiet neighborhoods, and great restaurants. There are tall hotels and office buildings. There are fancy stores, and wonderful museums. The Knesset, where Israel's laws are made, is there, too.

The eastern part of the city is called the Old City. It's surrounded by 450-year-old stone walls with eight huge gates. We walked on top of the 40-foot-high walls and took a peek into the Old City's four different neighborhoods—the Jewish Quarter, the Muslim Quarter, the Christian Quarter, and the Armenian Quarter.

Jerusalem

Hebrew, Arabic, English signs

رحوب الیهود

JEWISH QUARTER RD.

Old City entrance at Damascus Gate

Views of old and new Jerusalem

Jerusalem is a holy place to three major religions. It is holy to Jews because the city was the center of Judaism in Biblical days. Christians feel Jerusalem is holy because so many important events in Jesus' life took place here. Muslims believe that their prophet (teacher) Mohammed rose to heaven from Jerusalem to receive God's word.

Our guide told us that legend says when the leaves on Jerusalem's olive trees flutter in the breeze, God is breathing.

Jews and Judaism

Did you know that Jewish people in Israel (especially in Jerusalem) celebrate a holiday every Saturday? It's called Shabbat, or the Sabbath. It's a day of rest. Most Israelis are Jewish, so businesses are closed and buses don't run on the Sabbath.

The holiday begins at sunset on Friday evening. We dressed up and joined the crowds who gather for services in front of the Western Wall.

Prayers at the Western Wall

Devout Jews hurry to worship

Stained glass window

The Great Jerusalem Synagogue

Judaism is the world's oldest major religion. It was the first to teach the belief in one God, instead of many. The Western Wall is the holiest place in the Jewish world. Our tour guide explained that in the days of the Bible, the Holy Temple stood on the Temple Mount above this spot. But, the magnificent Temple was burned to the ground by Roman armies almost 2,000 years ago. All that was left was a courtyard wall.

Today the 50-foot high Wall is like a synagogue—that's a Jewish house of worship. People leave notes to God in the cracks between the Wall's rough stones. They also pray and celebrate holidays and special occasions there.

I can hardly wait until Sunday. We're going to walk in an underground tunnel beside the Great Wall!

9

Bar Mitzvah and Passover

One of the kids in our tour group became a bar mitzvah today! That's Hebrew for "son of the commandments." Now that he's 13, he is considered an "adult" member of the Jewish community. He is responsible for carrying out its laws and traditions.

Like Jews from all over the world, we went to the Wall for the ceremony. He read from the Torah, the first five books of the Old Testament. Then we threw candy at him! His Dad and the other men in our group made a circle around him and danced and sang. The women clapped along from the women's section.

Bar mitzvah ceremony

Bar mitzvah rites at the Western Wall

Traditional Passover seder meal

While we were there, Jews were getting ready to observe an important holiday called Passover. It's a springtime festival that remembers the ancient Israelites' escape from slavery in Egypt. As part of the holiday, families gather for a special dinner called a seder. This meal has lots of special foods in it. And each food is a symbol of something from the Passover story. As part of the seder, the Haggadah is read aloud. That's the story of the Jews' exodus (escape) from slavery in Egypt.

Muslims

On our first day here we saw a building with a beautiful golden dome glowing in the sunrise. Today we finally visited it!

The building is called the Dome of the Rock. It's a holy place for Muslims. Muslims are followers of Islam. They read from a holy book called the Koran and pray to Allah.

At the entrance to the building, there were hundreds of pairs of shoes! It's Muslim custom when entering a holy place to leave your shoes outside.

The inside and outside of this ancient, eight-sided building are decorated with fancy mosaics. Those are tile designs. The designs are patterns of shapes, flowers, and words from the Koran.

Muslim girls

Dome of the Rock

Dome of the Rock

Muslim girl riding a donkey

Muslim headcoverings on display in bazaar

We looked down at the huge, dark slab of rock in the center of the building. During Biblical times, the splendid Holy Temple stood over the rock. Our tour guide said that, according to Jewish tradition, it was upon this rock that Abraham—the father of the Jewish people—was prepared to sacrifice his son Isaac. Muslim's believe that Mohammed flew to heaven on his winged horse from this rock. For many Jews and Muslims, this rock is the center of the whole world!

Christians

Only a small number of Christians live in Israel, but hundreds of thousands of Christians from all over the world visit Jerusalem each year. That's because the city was home to Jesus Christ.

Today we joined a procession that has been going on every Friday afternoon for more than 600 years! We walked along the Via Dolorosa, or Walk of Sorrow. That's the path that Jesus took to his death. There are 14 stations, or places, on the path. People believe that each of these stations may have been where Jesus stopped to rest along the way. There is a church, a shrine, or a carving in stone marking each of these special places.

Christian procession on the Via Dolorosa

Coptic Egyptian priest at worship

Christian Easter service

Church of the Holy Selpuchre

Last Supper communion service

The procession ended in the Church of the Holy Sepulchre. This is one of Christianity's most sacred churches. The Church was built more than 850 years ago on the site where Jesus was crucified and buried. It was really quite an amazing thing to stand at this exact spot. Everywhere you go in this country, you're surrounded by the most incredible history!

In a few days, we'll be traveling to Bethlehem, where Jesus was born.

Daily Life

Kids in Israel go to school six days a week! Their day off depends on their religion. In Israel, most kids of different religions go to different schools.

Adults also work six days a week. Most city dwellers make a living in business, industry, or the building trades. Most cities have supermarkets, but many people like to shop at small neighborhood stores and open-air markets. We did, too!

Shoppers in Muslim Quarter

Spices on display in the market

Sheep outside old city walls

BANK OF ISRAEL
بنك إسرائيل

Israeli currency

Bagel cart

We joined the crowds in the busy souk—that's the market. We saw shop windows filled with bright goat-hair rugs, jewelry, wood carvings, and colorful embroidered clothing. The smell of spices and freshly baked pita bread and bagels made us really hungry.

There are lots of different kinds of restaurants to choose from. We finally stopped at a falafel stand for lunch. Falafel is Israel's favorite sandwich! It's a ball of chick peas that is fried golden and crispy. It's stuffed into a pita pocket along with chopped salad and a tasty sauce.

17

Bethlehem

We took a ten-minute bus ride south from Jerusalem to Bethlehem. Our guide said if we looked out the window we'd see what the city looked like when Jesus was alive—about 2,000 years ago. The city hasn't changed much since then! Shepherds still tend their flocks in the fields outside Bethlehem just like the shepherds in the Bible.

Shepherd's fields

Manger Square and Church of Nativity

Sign in Arabic and English

ساحة المهد

MANGER SQUARE

Shrine marking Jesus' birth

Mosaic of Jesus' Raising of Dead

Church altar

We headed to Manger Square and the 1,400-year-old Church of the Nativity. The church is built above the cave where Jesus was born. Caves were often used as barns in biblical times. In the middle of the white marble floor, a gleaming star with 14 points marks Jesus' birthplace. The points represent the Stations of the Cross that we walked on the Via Dolorosa in Jerusalem last week.

Tel Aviv-Jaffa

On Tuesday, we traveled 35 miles west by train from Jerusalem to Tel Aviv-Jaffa. That's Israel's second-largest city.

Tel Aviv-Jaffa is really two cities in one! Our guide explained that Jaffa was an important ancient port. Legend says it was named after Noah's son, Japhet. He supposedly founded it after the great flood waters fell back. Tel Aviv was founded less than a 100 years ago by Jewish families from Jaffa. Tel Aviv grew so quickly that the two cities became one in 1948. That's the same year Israel became a state.

Tel Aviv

Marinas and high rises in Tel Aviv

Tel Aviv-Jaffa is on the shores of the Mediterranean Sea, on Israel's western coast. The city is really busy! It's Israel's business and cultural center. The Israeli Stock Exchange and the world's largest diamond-polishing industry are located here.

Today we visited the noisy, crowded Carmel Market. Stalls were bursting with colorful fruits and vegetables grown outside the city on the warm, fertile coast.

It's hard to believe that less than 100 years ago the city was only sand dunes, because now Tel Aviv-Jaffa has everything!

Haifa and Nazareth

Today, we left Tel Aviv-Jaffa and traveled about 50 miles north along the coast to Haifa. On our way, we stopped at some excellent beaches! The one at Caesarea was especially beautiful. That was between Tel-Aviv and Haifa.

Like Tel Aviv, Haifa was built less than 100 years ago. Its modern harbor makes it Israel's most important port. It is also a heavy manufacturing area. Oil refineries, factories, mills, and ship builders are located here.

Haifa has fancy hotels, two universities, a zoo, and the only subway in all of Israel! We visited the beautiful terraced gardens of the golden-domed Bahai Temple. The temple is the headquarters for the Bahai faith. Bahai followers believe that some day there will be one religion, one language, and peace among all humankind.

Tel Aviv-Jaffa coastline

Bahai Temple

Basilica of the Annunciation

Basilica of the Annunciation

After two days exploring Haifa, we boarded the bus for our trip southeast to Nazareth. Our guide explained that Nazareth was where Jesus spent his childhood and where he first began to preach.

When we got there we headed for the Basilica of the Annunciation. It's the largest church in the Middle East! It is the fifth church to stand on the site of Mary's house. Christian tradition teaches that an angel appeared here to tell Mary she would give birth to the son of God.

River Jordan and the Galilee

From Nazareth we took the bus east through the lower Galilee region toward Tiberias.

We're using Tiberias, one of Judaism's four holy cities, to explore the area around the Sea of Galilee.

Our guide said the Sea of Galilee, in northeastern Israel, is probably the world's most famous lake! It was on the Sea of Galilee that Jesus is said to have walked.

Mosaic of miracle of loaves and fishes

River Jordan

Ancient Christian mosaic

We took a ferry boat ride from Tiberias to Capernaum. There, Jesus found his first apostles—his first followers. They were working as fishermen. According to the guide book, Jesus preached more sermons and performed more miracles at Capernaum than anywhere else. On a hillside east of the city he preached the famous Sermon on the Mount. In nearby Tabgah, he is said to have multiplied 5 loaves of bread and 2 fish into enough food to feed 5,000 hungry people who had come to hear him speak.

The River Jordan is Israel's longest and most important river. It comes from the Sea of Galilee. Because Jesus was baptized, or cleansed, in the Jordan, many pilgrims come to its banks to pray, sing, and bathe.

Galilee

We're spending two days in a guest house on the shores of Lake Kinneret—that's the Hebrew name for the Sea of Galilee.

Besides being the birthplace of Christianity, the area around Lake Kinneret is where the world's first kibbutz was founded. A kibbutz is a group farm. Some have guest houses where you can stay. We stayed at one right near the water.

After a big breakfast in the huge cafeteria, we got a tour from one of the kibbutz members.

Wildflowers in Galilee

Sunrise over Sea of Galilee

Teaching inside Kibbutz

Kibbutz

Church ruins

She explained that a kibbutz is like a big family. Everyone works together for the good of the group and shares the results. People have different jobs—from driving tractors to teaching in the kibbutz school. Kids have jobs, too. But, instead of making their beds, they work in the garden or feed the chickens! Kids don't get allowances. Parents don't get paychecks. The kibbutz pays for everything its members need—from clothing and education to medical care and vacations.

Dead Sea and Masada

This morning, we got up before sunrise so we could climb the "Snake Path" to Masada before it got too hot. Masada is a huge, flat-topped rock. It rises 1,000 feet from the middle of the Judean Desert, southeast of Jerusalem. At the top are the ruins of a 2,000-year-old palace fort.

I thought I'd be tired of seeing more ruins, but the amazing story our guide told us changed my mind.

View from fort at Masada

Cable car to Masada

Mosaic on Masada floor

Dead sea marker

הנקודה הנמוכה ביותר בעולם
394 מתר מתחת לפני ה ט
أوطأ نقطة في العالم ٣٩٤م تحت سطح البحر
THE LOWEST POINT ON
EARTH 394 M BELOW SEA
LEVEL

Around A.D. 70, there was a war between the Romans and the Jews. A group of Jewish warriors and their families retreated to Masada after Jerusalem fell to the enemy. They refused to surrender for two years. They even built a synagogue at the site. Finally, the Romans brought 15,000 soldiers to battle the fewer than 1,000 Jewish rebels. After a long battle, it became clear that the Romans would capture the fortress. Rather than surrender and live as slaves, the Jews burned their camp and killed themselves and their children. Masada has since become a symbol of Jewish courage and determination.

After our hot, dry morning at Masada, I could hardly wait to go swimming in the nearby Dead Sea. Was I surprised! The Dead Sea is the lowest place on Earth. Forget a cool swim—the warm water is so salty, you can't sink. Nothing can live in it—not fish or plants. That's how it got its name.

Qumran and Dead Sea Scrolls

At a really cool museum in Jerusalem we saw the oldest known copies of the Old Testament. Today, we saw where they were hidden. They had been sitting in caves for more than 2,000 years!

Our guide told us they were found in 1947 by a young shepherd looking for a lost goat. Instead, he found the scrolls tucked into large clay jars and hidden deep in a cave.

Caves at Qumran

The scrolls, now known as the Dead Sea Scrolls, belonged to a community of very religious Jews. They lived in the wilderness near the shores of the Dead Sea. The scrolls included almost all of the books of the Old Testament, as well as texts of prayers, songs, and laws.

Glossary

Baptize to pour water on someone's head as a sign that he or she is becoming a Christian.

Fertile condition of land that is good for growing crops.

Mosaic a picture or pattern made up of small pieces of colored glass, tile, or stone.

Pilgrim someone who journeys to worship at a holy place.

Prophet a person who speaks, or claims to speak, from God.

Sacred holy, deserving great respect.

Seder a ceremonial dinner held at a Jewish home on the first night of Passover to commemorate the exodus from Egypt.

Shrine a holy building that often contains sacred objects.

Synagogue a building used by Jewish people for religion or study.

For More Information

Books

Bailey, Donna. Anna Sproule. *Israel* (Where We Live). Chatham, NJ: Steck-Vaughn Library Division, 1990.

Bickman, Connie. *Children of Israel* (Through the Eyes of Children). Minneapolis, MN: Abdo & Daughters, 1994.

Web Sites

Facts About Israel

See what aspects of Israeli education, sports, and culture are different from or the same as those in North America—www.israel-mfa.gov.il/facts.

Focus on Israel

Discover more about this country's climate, language, government and way of life—www.focusmm.com.au/israel/is_tu_01.htm.

Index